the pickle in the middle presents

SELF-SABOTAGE

with a
side of  GLITTER

JANA SALVATORE

I0521773

SYNERGY
PUBLISHING GROUP

BELMONT, NORTH CAROLINA

The Pickle in the Middle Presents:
Self Sabotage with a Side of Glitter

Jana Salvatore

Published by Synergy Publishing Group, Belmont, NC
Layout and design by Melisa Graham

Softcover, February 2026, ISBN 978-1-960892-58-4
Ebook, February 2026, ISBN 978-1-960892-61-4

Dedication

For the beautifully off-kilter part of you that never stops whispering the truth, even when you try to ignore it while it is screaming at you.

Remember, you are never too much, too weird, or not enough. Keep sharing your love and shining your light.

Contents

write on me

Hey you,

I see you stepping back, hiding in your room, peeking out from behind that curtain. You may be wanting to disappear or escape from the world and your life.

It is feeling heavy. It is feeling lonely. Overwhelming.

When in reality, you really want someone to find you. Seek you out. You are searching for a purpose. A sense of belonging. You want things to be the way they once were. A simpler time.

You want to get out of this dark place, but you aren't sure how or where to begin. Or, if you get out of the dark, you may be unsure of how to remain in this better place.

It can often feel better to stay where you are because changing can be difficult. Right? It can be downright scary. But there is a better way.

If you are ready to stop peering out from behind the curtain and disappearing from the world ... I found you.

Let's go on a journey together to bring you back into alignment with who you are meant to be. Let's discover the things you want to do in order to live purposefully, love abundantly, and laugh joyfully.

As you read through this book, look at it as a journey of your own self-discovery. It is to be interactive. Write in the margins! Write on the blank pages interspersed throughout the book!

write in the margins

Ask yourself ...

* Is this provoking something internally within me?
* Which poem do I want to use as a journal entry today?
* What thoughts are coming forward?
* Where am I noticing this in my body?
* Did it provoke a deep thought, an experience?
* Did it make me mad, uneasy?
* Did it make me smile, laugh?
* Did it make me say, "Heck yes! I resonate with this"?

Express how you need to express.

Embody what you need to embody.

Embrace whatever comes through.

Write, draw, dance, sing, scream, really belt it out however that looks for you!

My personal journey has made me realize that had I not had the many tools in my toolbox, things could have turned out far bleaker for me. As a coach and mentor, I help others create their own toolboxes and be their own *soft* landing. I bring forward the patterns that I notice. I guide others on a journey of self-discovery and self-awareness, to bring clarity and joy in all they do.

Please know this: Even when your life throws you curveballs, you can still move forward. The setback doesn't define you; it is the catalyst for your next chapter. Your new timeline.

What will define you is how you choose your way forward. Your comeback. Wherever you are at any given moment in your life is okay. We are living a human experience. Feel it. Own it. Be it.

Happy journeying,
Jana

P.S. I'm sure you are wondering about the pickle on the cover of the book. The pickle is a visual metaphor for the disruption or the catalyst needed for change. It can be good. It can be bad. It can be infuriating. It can be hilarious. The pickle represents the moment in the journey you are on in life. It will be a staple within my writings. Fun and playful. Irritating and deep.

PART I

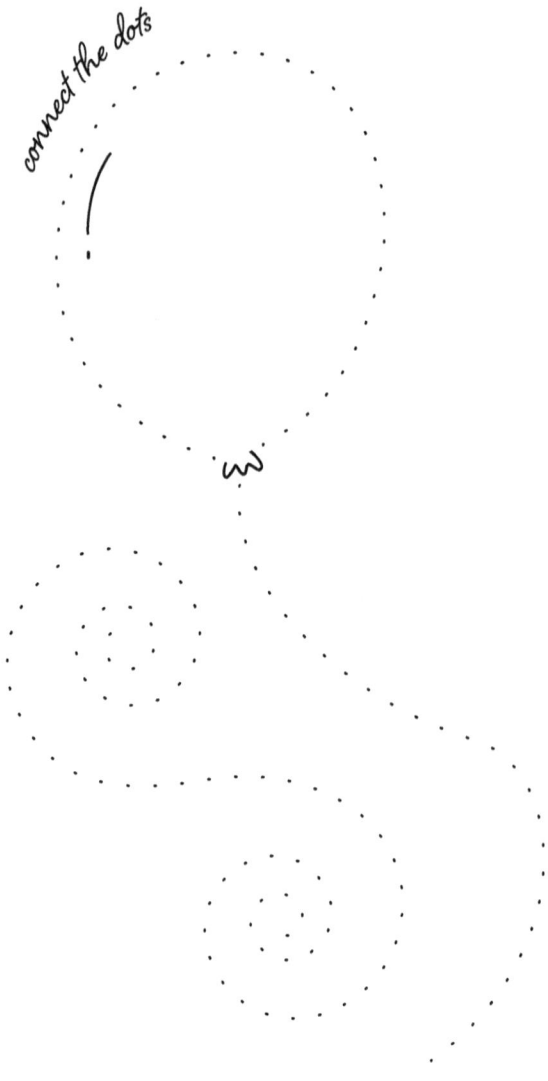

connect the dots

Writing My Way Through

My thoughts

What is wanting to come through me today?
Tired
Shit-show between the shit-sandwich
And the jam to make it better

Stories for my younger self

Writing is my therapy
Clunky to clarity
Bumpy to bouncy
Transaction in the transformation
Duality
Grieving to gratitude
Different forms of grieving

You are the priority
My journey of grief, guilt, people-pleasing and losing
myself again
Reclaiming what I found
and lost
in a matter of a month
Duality of life
Boundaries
Worthiness

Breaking point
God doesn't give you what you can't handle
I want to return to sender

I can't make this shit up

Is it worth it?
Journey into relationships of self,
spouse,
family,
others

Being the scapegoat and the target
for others so they can justify
treating you badly.
Being tired of the projections of others
relationship dynamics
When others can't see
you as someone different

Being pigeonholed to an old identity
by others who cannot move past the past ...
because they would need to admit
and own that their words and actions
have deteriorated relationships
My relationships with certain people

You can only extend an olive branch so much
Dealing with their own guilt and shame
Can't see their own dysfunction

Letting go of expectations

Acceptance of self
and others
Stepping back

The tension I've held in my body ...
beginning to release
I can feel the results
good and bad

Jaws, chest, shoulders ...

The hurt to slowing down and breathing
It's okay to rest
The last breath—dad—"I took her last breath"

The masks we wear
The doors we walk through each day
Merging into wholeness

The empty seat at the table
The meals we eat
The games we play
What are we eating?

The Words on the Paper Are Screaming ...

I am grounded into curiosity and possibility.
Allowing life to unfold as it needs to,
in order to flow.
I trust the process and what it is guiding me to.
Who I am to become?
The words on the paper are screaming ...
What do they want to say?
What do they *need* to say?
So much inside. The words are jumbled.
The clarity is far, yet so near?
How to prioritize what to bring forward ...
When in reality ...
no prioritizing is needed.
Allow it to flow!
No restrictions!
No reservations!
No resistance!
The plates I am carrying,
the space I am holding,
for myself,
for others.
Nurturing myself as I move through the grief process.
The nurturing of my heart from spouse's heart surgery.
The preparation for a huge move and moving to our

dream home.
Plates are spiraling.
Some are crashing!
Some are spinning!
The plates that are crashing,

$\mathcal{I}$ released the control!
The ones that are spiraling,
are in my grasp to release or accept.
The ones that are spinning are humming to a beat of
their own,
Whispering quietly and moving forward.
Then there are the still the ones ...
the counter balance if you will.
They hold the tipping point.
They hold the balance,
of my heart
my mind
my soul
my spirit
Do they spin?
Do they spiral?
Or do they crash out of control?
Where is forgiveness necessary?
Where is acceptance required?
Where in this is compassion the answer?
Where is the grace you are lending to yourself?
Where is the celebration and the brightness?
The joy and the gratitude.
The laughter and the freedom.

Freedom to live in the contrast,
No limitations on light and dark,
happy and sad,
expansion and contraction,
the high and the low.
Just to be.
Be in the moment,
that is now.
To be present,
to observe
to live
to celebrate
me
Who I am!
Who I was!
Who I will become!

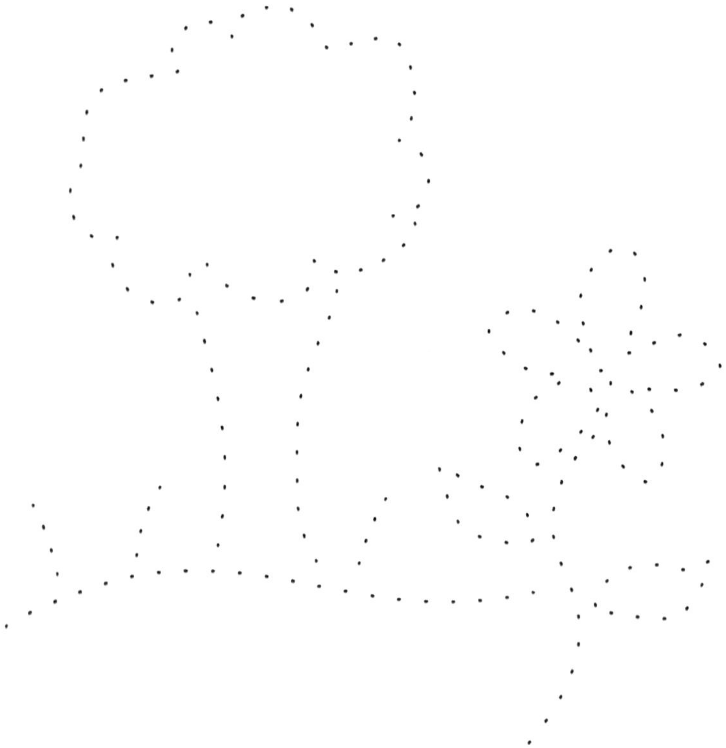

Shower Wisdom

Shake it up!
What do I need/want in order to thrive?
What needs to change?
What do I need to own?
Where in my body do I feel all of this?
What is it saying to me?
What needs to go?
Shift?

Empowered beginnings!
Neurodivergent/adhd/tbi!

Removing the masks,
Time to glow up!
Consistency.
What does that even mean
... to me,
A dreamer,
A free spirit?

Why am I so awesome?
From idiocracy to mediocrity to curiosity

The ego is in control ... so it thinks.
Anxiety and overwhelm.
What are the voices saying?

What is that sucker punch telling me?
My gut said what?

Feeling outside of me,
Cycle of change
Seasons of life
Seasons of the year
I am a seasonal being
Paying attention to the patterns and signs.

What surprises me?
I'm proud of me!
Being the soft landing for others.

Guiding others in creating
a soft landing for themselves
during hard times
and preparing themselves for success.

Punitive self-love.
Conditional love and action.
Bravery/Courage through threat of failure
and success.

What needs to blow up to glow up?
It's all about curiosity!

Consistency thriving in the chaos and doubt
is where I shine
How to tame it?

How to imperfectly plant my flag
and commit to my truth and power?
The thing I fear
is the thing I must do
Cold heart warm feet
Cold feet warm heart
Hormones from hell and the confusion that goes with
it—menopausal journey

What is filling my blank space

Shower wisdom and musings
Self-doubt swirling down the drain

My DNOS (Dark Night of the Soul) Phase

Still waters run deep
Sabbatical
I accomplished what I needed to
What have I achieved
Loneliness
Enjoy being alone
Solitude
Misery to bliss
Squeeze every ounce of happiness out of solitude
Explore curiosity
What you are determining your growth
Unbalanced chakras series
What is excelling in the stillness
Values
Inspiration, creativity, trust, love, connection, truth

Get through it to be it
Mini retreats for family
Using my higher self and art to guide my business
Unclog the dam, knock it down
Intuition is more powerful than limited beliefs
My year of simplicity
Ease and things that are easy and light
Increase resistance or Increase allowing

What is my personal geometry
Security comes from within
Stop connecting to other people's maps
You are your own divine being
Stay in your own reality
When lonely, not connecting to your higher self
Doesn't need to be all or nothing

Finding footing, creating my cobblestone path

Honor resistance
Reassurance breaks

Okay to be there
just don't stay there
Foundational pieces
Boundaries
I am a creative being
Plant the seeds
Unnecessary pressures that are self made
What can we do to press pause now
Be our own 911 operator
Spiritual decluttering/clear our own hardware
Chanting
Look at the battlefield in a new way

Life Gets to be Messy

It gets to be clean
It gets to be pristine
It gets to be testy

Make it what you want
Make it what you don't want
You get to chose
You chose to win
You chose to lose

And in the end—win or lose—you win
You learn the lessons
You cry on your terms
You sing when you want
You dance to celebrate

Life gets to be messy!
Life *is* messy!
It isn't perfect.
And if you think others are perfect,
think again.

Some are pretending
Others are struggling
Some are happy to be vertical
Some are sad yet moving forward

Some are choosing their hard
Some are choosing their easy

Life gets to be messy in how we choose it.
It's your life!
You decide your messiness each day.

The Conundrum of Grief and Joy

We are conditioned to believe
That if we are grieving
We shouldn't have joy in our lives.

How can you be laughing when your loved one
just died!
You should be grieving
You should be doing this or that

I say screw that.

I am grieving. I have been grieving for many years over
various things ...

But most recently, my mom.
She passed unexpectedly
January 31st.
The day is a blur.
One big freaking blur.

12 hours of twists and turns
Heartbreak and heartache

As I'm navigating the grief journey,
one thing is for sure ...
I know that my mom would not want us to sit and

do nothing.
She would want us to continue living our lives.
Find the joy moments.
Laugh.
LIVE.

We can still be grieving and have fun.
We can still be grieving and find our joy.
By doing this, we are celebrating our loved ones.

We love deeper
We live more intentionally
We laugh harder

My focuses have shifted.

Art of Creation

It encompasses all areas of our lives
From cooking to cleaning
To painting to sculpting
To raising your family
To how you organize your drawers

So many people are of the mindset
that creativity is only art creation

What if art is your life?
You are the artist, the brush per se
Your life is your canvas

Add color where you need it
Add contrast to deepen or illuminate
Highlight for shining
Contour for depth

So much to create
So much to innovate
So much to invigorate

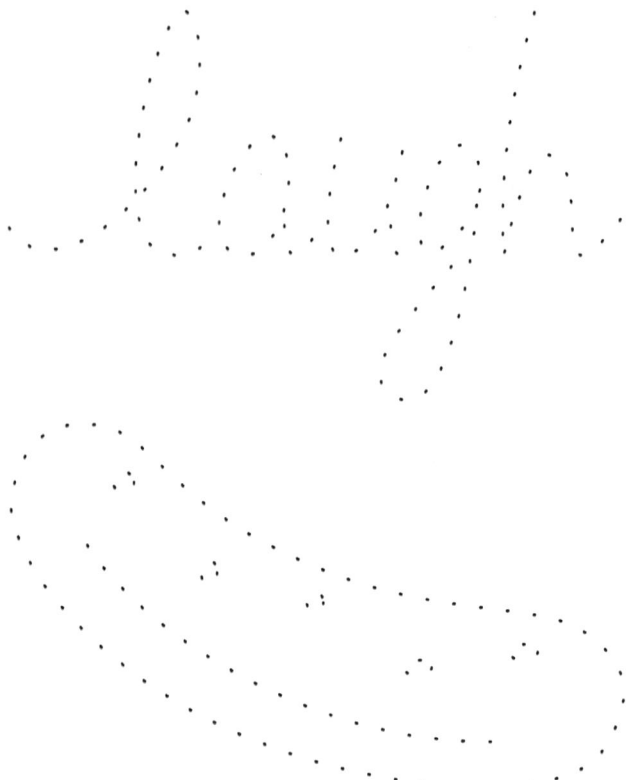

Sensitivity is my Superpower

Soar
Embrace
Nurture
See
Intertwine
Totality
Integration
Veracity
Innovation
Tenacious
Yearning ...

Energy Within to Energy Without
or
Energy Without to Energy Within?

Soaring
Flying
Creating
Flowing
Easeful
Living
No longer
Sinking
Flailing
Blocked
Locked
Shutdown
Exhausted
....

Seeing the light
Not the dark
Seeing the forest
Not the trees
Seeing the stars
Not the clouds
Seeing the shimmers
And the glimmers

Pickle no more

For the pickle
Will surface
To trip you up
To sabotage your path
Your journey
Your joy
For it is within you
To squelch the pickle
And turn it into
Glimmers
Shimmers
And Joy

Cocooning

Cocooning to rejuvenate
To emerge restored
To release what's no more
To release expectations
To release what was
Cocooning for self-preservation
To begin a transformation
To be the butterfly
No longer the caterpillar
Or the larvae
But if not for the larvae
the others would not soar and transform
Chrysalis no more

See the beauty in the process
embrace the moments
embrace the suck
for the
release of these
moments
instead of resisting
will free your mind
your body
your soul

It will give you strength

It will give you clarity
It will give you peace
It will give you energy!

Mind

I will allow the thoughts to come forward
I will hold what is necessary
I will delete what is not
I will feel the thoughts in my body
For it is my compass

Embody what serves me
Release what does not

And for the thoughts that repeat
I will ask who is that?
Is it spirit?
Is it human?
Is it animal?

Embody what serves me
Release what does not

I will do my checks and balances
And make the choice to hold on to it or not

For I am my champion
My voice is hope
My heart is love
My soul is light

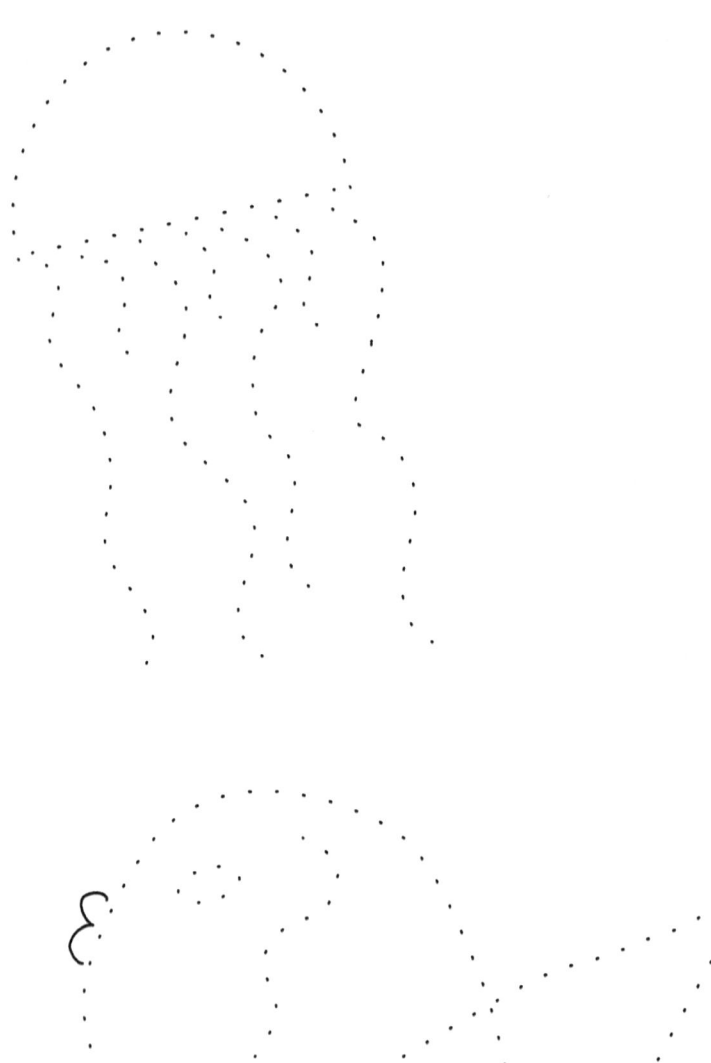

Body

My body speaks volumes
It shouts
And it cowers
It contracts and it expands
It's warm and it's frigid
It's rigid and it's soft

It shows me where
I need to focus
Healing
Loving
Creation
Letting go
Grounding
Truth telling
Connection
Certainty

It drains me when I'm overdoing it
It energizes me when I'm on fire
It drains me when I'm misaligned
It energizes me when I shine

It energizes me when I serve
To my highest good

It shows me the pain
I need to release
It shows me the areas
To integrate

It shows me the areas
Of perpetual self-abuse

It shows me the areas
Of solidifying truths

It shares with me the hopes and dreams
That were actualized and shattered

It protects me from fears
It pads me from shining

It is a choice to be
Gentle or kind

The bowl full of jelly
Rumbles and rolls

For it was for protection
Self-preservation

Goals unachieved
Feeling deceived
Societal and familial pressurized
Sabotage activated

Self-esteem tattered
Self-worth shattered

Dreams be gone
Mundane outdone

To grapple in truth
Facing the demons ensued
To bring to reality
Clarity of worth
For I was on earth
No longer in the realm
Of effervescence and shine
Spirit and human are now intertwined

Mind Body Declutter Challenge

What are you seeing in the gray?
Bright colors,
Richer tones,
Not so much the gloom,
Adjust the thoughts to see a different perspective ...

What is needing to shift today?

PART II

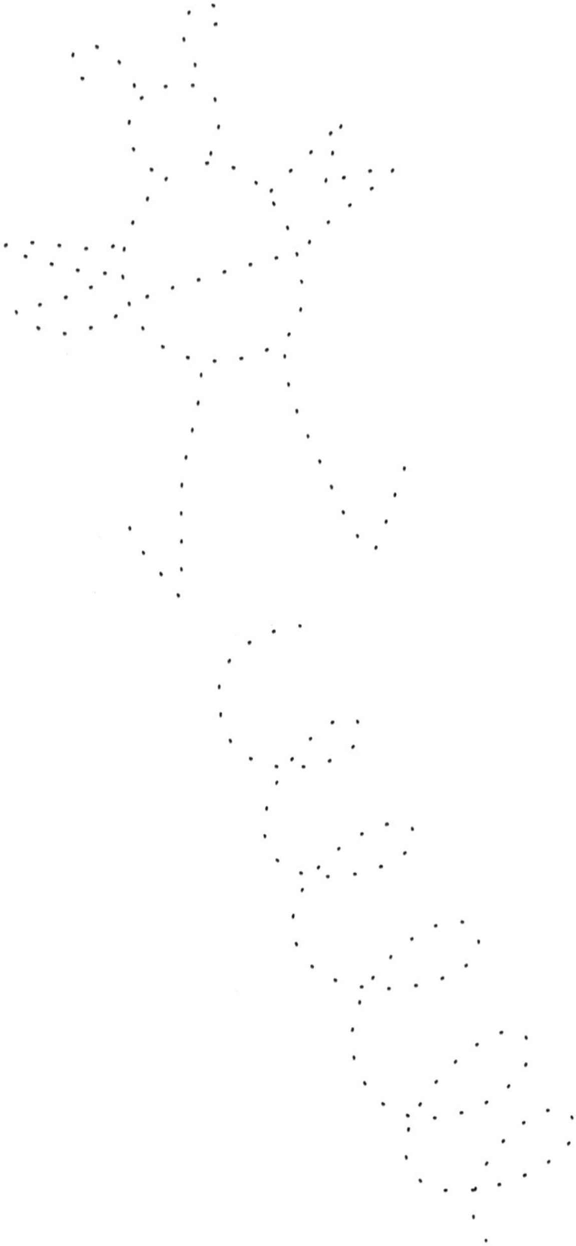

Needy Baby, Greedy Baby

In the stillness the ego dies
Being at one with our mind, our body and soul
Breathes new life and a new dawn

Wish I may
Wish I might
Breathe in a new life tonight

The shimmers fall about on the lake top
The sun is reflecting a new static of electricity.
A new current
You can see the shift of the current
The direction of flow
An ease of comfort
For it to show
A new way
A new path
What is beneath the current is a deeper depth
A whole new life of activity
Sight unseen and true
For what is above is not always so below
Below is activity
The turmoil
The battles
The thoughts
The attachments

The beliefs

What you see above the surface in not always what
is below
The cracking is muted to hide
The pain
The fear
The envy the jealousy
The excitement
The contentment
The joy
As above so below ... on the surface not below
The depths of the current.

As above and so below
The shimmers the glimmers on the surface

The ripple of the current as the wind blows over it
As above is not below
What's below is depth
A swirl
The life we don't see
Birthing of anew

Rising Above the Mess

Change locations!
Move when feeling bad.
River banks, it's not deep at the sides.
Do not lose faith!
Shake off resistances!
Swirls are getting rid of the crap,
You can't bring the baggage to paradise!
Move to feel better.
We are here to live out our fantasies!
Wear sunscreen if you need it.

Exasperation in the Exhale

I breathe in.
I breathe out.
Hesitation with a hiccup in the inhale
Exasperation in the exhale
What if this happens and it all goes wrong
BUT
What IF this happens and it all goes right
Find the courage
Feel the flutters
Release the tightness
Release the grip
I feel it slipping
Reel it back in
Hold it tight
Breathe in
Breathe out
It will be alright.

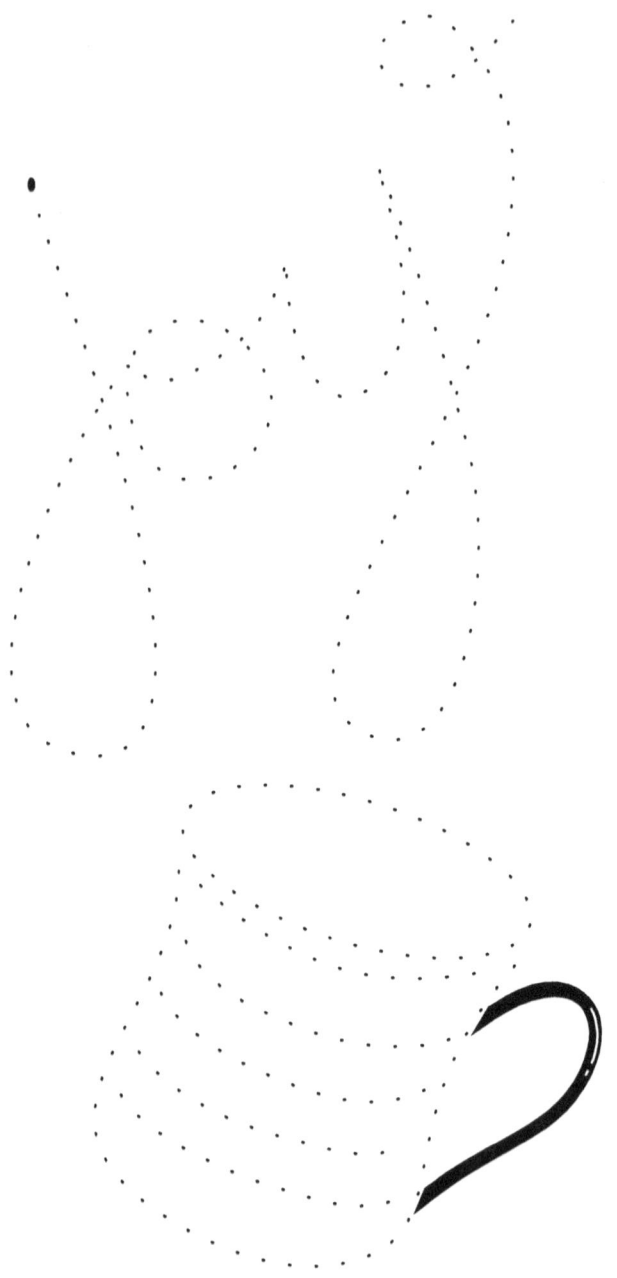

Anxiety No More

Overwhelm brought clarity
Judgment schmugment
Take the break. Take the walk.

You're human, relax
Live the human experience!

About the Thermostat

4AM Thoughts
No! Not again
It's 4AM
I'm awake
Tossing
Turning
Mind racing
Hot flash
Toss the covers
Wait! Now I'm cold
Cover back up
Damn it.
HOT HOT HOT
The cycle continues ...

I fell asleep at 2AM
And here it is 4AM
Time to rise
And write a poem
About the thermostat
That is malfunctioning within
Sending me into the throes of hell
The inferno
Only
To catapult me
To the Arctic

Freezing, shivering
Wide awake
Rolling the eyes
Groans of annoyance
Thirsty
Clammy
Menopause ...

Create the Damn Boxes

Filling the voids in our heart, mind and soul
Are you ready to let it go ... Hold on to it longer
I don't want to let it go. You can't make me.
IF I release what I'm holding onto ...
what will fill that space?
Easier to hold on to the negative
than to feel and release them
Is it a real or false sense of safety?
Creating a new foundation can be scary
Spiraling out of control
Spiraling into alignment
"Whoa is me!" to "How do I navigate this?"
SNOWGLOBE SHAKE UP
What is important?
Different perspectives for people
Here to make an impact
Conversation with me and my homies

Feeling guilty for feeling relief

Create the damn boxes

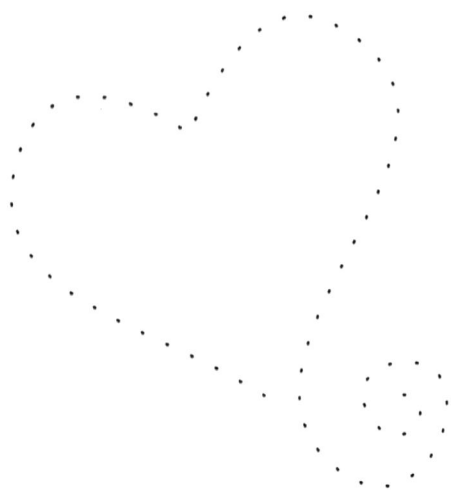

Love Notes for Today

What does my heart need now?
I'll never get it right
if I'm out of alignment.

Let's shift one thing.
Joy, check.
What do you need?
Possibility poker?
Let's be honest
I'm in coping mode.

Surround yourself with the right people
Although,
the wrong people
lead you to the right people!

What is my intuitive process?
What is my signature process?

Misalignment Release

I love you ... I RELEASE you

I forgive you ... I forgive MYSELF

Thank you for teaching me who to become
I am ready for myself at the next level

I thank you I bless you

I release any energies and emotions that are not mine

I open the power of my heart and let it shine upon my
life and others.

What am I ready for?

What do I want to experience in my next life?

Which aspects of myself have been hidden,
dormant or buried
and that may be ready
to come to the surface
in a bigger way?

Is this the year?

Am I ready to release any energies and emotions that are not mine?

Shimmering Shadows

The shimmers and glimmers,
The glitz and glam
The wax and the shine
All for a moment in time.

Behind closed doors,
The sheen turns murky
The sparkles demure
The shine is for show
The shadow endures.

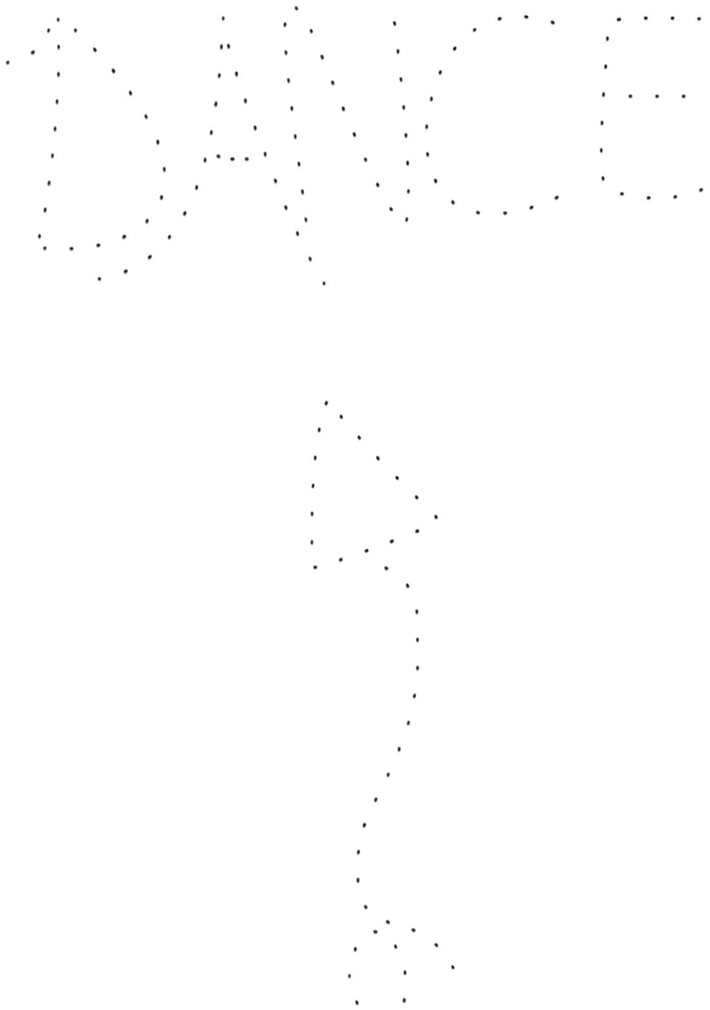
DANCE

Self-Sabotage with a Side of Glitter

Layers shake loose
resistance fades away
Harmonious sense of relief and joy
Sabotage with a side of glitter sparkling in
Confidence coming forward
Chest is a little tight. Head kicking in
Aura is soft and pastel colored
The netting is sparkling and bright
Certainty is coming in.
My right foot is feeling a soft cinder block.
Move forward, kick it high
The ribbon is flowing freely
Expanding
Colorful light swirling around
Path/purpose is coming alive
Surviving is no longer the word
thriving is a current
feeling alive is ignited
deep within my core
shining brightly
dimming now more
the fireworks are colorful
the intentions are clear
the impact is charged
the mission is here
burn it down

to build it up
blow up
to glow up
the layers have faded
the conscience is clear
the heart is full
the heart is open
the soul is smoldering
the soul in emboldened
shining the light
sharing the gifts
bringing the dreams
of full confidence
no more resistance
no more confrontation
the wonderment is flourishing
free
expansive
the shackles are released
the chains are broken
My legs are weightless
My arms are flowing
My mind is open
My heart is receiving
I am allowing
I am being
I am flowing
I am a channel
I am a beacon
I am a vessel

I am a voice
Power
Clarity
Inspiration
Joy
Laughter
Hope
Guidance
Love

PART 3

Today, Do No Damage

No Damage you say
but I'm in the fray!
The fray of my thoughts
my feelings
my emotions.
I'm not able to control!
I don't want to be tame,
I like the drama
The chaos
emotions bring.
The upheaval is set into motion,
The catalyst of change is here.
I'm here to be shocking,
a force to the status quo,
to guide others to see clearer,
to find their own voice!
The damage is collateral
for change.
It often dismantles the foundations
of what was once believed,
our core identities
are shattered
and pieces put back together
in
a mosaic of colors,
of broken parts,

mended and smoothed.
The transparency!
The sheen!
The scars endured!

The wisdom that comes forward
to the wise old owl
to oversee what is around
and share with crowds that surround.

Rock

the Rock is stability
that shoulders the burdens
the Rock holds me up
when things unravel
when the Rock falls down
my heart shatters
for my stability is withered
my soul withdrawn
it's in this moment
that I recognize
my Rock is support

For
I am the Foundation
and in turn
my time is now
to become the rock for my Rock
and shoulder the burdens
to be the beacon of light
to rise above
to ignite

for this is only temporary
my Rock will soon rise
we will intertwine
our strength will empower

for now is the time
to support not cower

Confetti

I am coming back into myself
Being
Coming home
Uniting with my heart
My sacral
Igniting a new way forward
Connecting on a deeper level
Feeling the warmth and the fire
Burning and yearning
To be birthed
Acknowledged
Loved
To celebrate
To dance
The beauty of contentment
The silence is golden
The stillness is profound
Peace being made
Internally
Externally
Swirling around
In a beautiful spiral
Of color
And confetti
Sparkles
And shimmers

The light is turning brighter
The darkness is extinguished
Heaviness has been lifted
In this moment I am free
Free to be me
Free to express
My feelings
My heart
My fears
My love
My sorrows
My joy
My anger
My peace
My happiness
Supersedes my melancholy
Compassion in the mess
The murkiness of my life
I feel the muck falling off
Of my shell
The stoic self
Is softening
Is listening
Is tuning into
And shutting out the noise
Bringing clarity
And calm
Peace and solace
Comfort
Gratitude

Openness to my heart
The expansion is grounding
Deep in my root
Into the ground
Rooting me into
A sense of safety
And security
To be grounded into the depths of
my heart
my soul
my desires
my purpose
my love
of self
of others
of community
of nurturing
my family
my animals
my friends
my community
myself
for I am the tree that is
planted firmly
grounded
strong
and waiting for the next storm
to come through
to knock me over
and do it all over again.

And each time the rebuild and rebirth
Is quicker
Sturdier
Stronger
And
Fierce
For one day, I will not be knocked off kilter
and will remain where planted
My voice, strength and courage
will be heard from where I stand
not where I search
the love, compassion and gratitude
I have for myself and others
Will shine through where I'm planted
For others to bloom and
Embody the wisdom I've shared
Through the challenges
The joys
The sadness
The happiness
The frustration
The contentment
The stillness
The comfort
The love
For I am now home

Who Are "They"?

"They" say there is strength in numbers
Who is "they"?
"They" say ask for help
Who is "they?"
And then,
I look for the numbers.
I ask for the help

"They" say I am needy
Who is "they?"

Is the Wine Okay?

Enjoying the day. The date.
Spending time with my spouse
Wine tasting music
Communication connection
To reconnect for a brief moment
As life got in the way
Surgery, death, illness, injury, building, moving
And now an accident
Rear-ended at 50 mph
Hold on hold on
My husbands yells
I watch in the side view mirror
I relax and close
My eyes as
I melt into the headrest
Knowing in a matter of seconds the impact was near ...
Screeching
Boom, crack
The sound
Reverberates through the car
My new car.
My mind races to
The ass of the car is not in the backseat so that's good
Is the wine okay? I'm not wearing red, white, or glass.

Priorities.

Love of my Life Or
Life of my Love

An Anniversary Poem for My Love on 9-19-2024

It feels like we met before
Meeting in the ethers
to play
to dance
to love

intertwining in the cosmos
creating
dreaming
being free

free to be who
we are meant to be
when we meet
in 3D

instant connection
it felt
as we met
the giant teddy bear
turned into my frog prince
to my rock

the love is pure and real
not tainted and calculated
the challenges
connect us deeper
to our core
a deeper layer uncovered each day
to reconnect us to the ethers
where we dance
play
love
intertwining
creating
dreaming
being free
free to be
who we are meant
to be
in 3D

Energy Vampires and Abundance

Pop up
Dump in
Drop in
Spirit has its way of showing up!

Ten days of gratitude
Invites abundance!

There are
Energy vampires in our lives
So
We PLAY in the boredom!

Excelling in stillness.
The Universe is fun!
Be the observer in your life!
Stop hoarding joy,
Step over the trash
Have fun

EPILOGUE

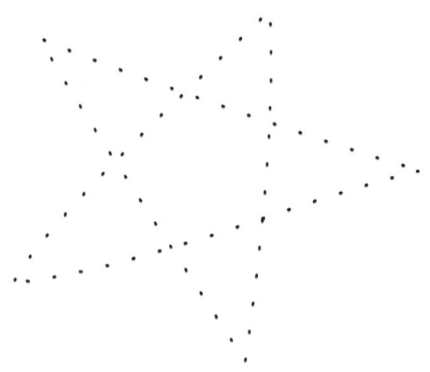

How am I Receiving Today?

Musings from this morning's meetup
Similar themes
Presence, stillness, flow
Frustration and anger—blessings
What's behind the flutter?

What would Gram do?
Excelling in the stillness
First thought/ first word

How am I receiving today?

....

How am I receiving?
Throughout my writing of this book, I have noticed
various themes and where my mind goes in the face
of disruption.
Hence the name *Self Sabotage with a Side of Glitter*
Throughout this process, I have learned many ways
to receive.
In love
In loss
In chaos
In calm
All bring me back to gratitude
And serving
Myself

Others
Being kind
Caring
And
Compassionate
While also realizing and accepting that it is okay to be where you are in those disruptive and crappy moments. We are human. We are here to feel the feelings, learn the lessons, release what no longer serves us and accept that some things will remain the same. We do so by not allowing it to consume us or become part of our identities.
Understanding that these are moments.
And these moments
Are not our identities.
You are not your mistakes.
You were experimenting and learning
What works and what doesn't
You are a beautiful human living a human experience.

In my receiving now, there tend to be similar themes.

Presence, stillness, flow are the ultimate goal.
Frustration and anger—find the blessings and gratitude.
Ask yourself, "What's behind the flutter, the disruption, the pickle?"
What need isn't being met by yourself or others?
Are you mad at yourself?

How can you excel in the stillness?

Acknowledge the first thought,first word that is
coming forward as you check in with your heart
Close your eyes, take a deep breath in, and listen
Listen to your heart
The quiet that surrounds you
The whisper that comes forward
And ask
How am I receiving today?

Sharing my journey with you is meant to inspire you
and hopefully help to mend your mind, body, soul,
and heart!

About Jana Salvatore

I walk the talk. I lead with courage, bravery and strength.

I have bad days. Some ... really ... bad days.

I have good days. I have freaking amazing days

I have days where I cry. I grieve. I grieve the loss of my mom, my animals, relatives and lost friendships. I grieve a life of what was or could have been. The parts of me that I wish were still here and the parts of me that were not self.

But these moments have taught me so much about myself, life, and others. And most of all these moments have taught me about love, gratitude, acceptance, peace, and understanding.

As a coach, I don't bring forward toxic positivity. I'm not a sugar coater. I'm real. I'm quirky. I'm raw. When we work together in my container of support, I will inspire you.

I will guide you. I will honor who and where you are and move you forward to the next level of where you want to go. Who you want to become. I bring knowledge, trainings, life experiences. I lead with love. I uncover truth. I allow you to shine. I provide a safe space. I will push you when necessary.

Ultimately the journey is yours to transform. Transform into who you want to become.

Where you want to go. How you want to lead.

Acknowledgments

Writing this book was equal parts joy, excavation, fear, and miracle. Probably more fear than anything. I could not have done it without the people who held me through every rise, fall, and the resistance. Oh, the resistance.

This book had its own attitude, deadlines, tantrums … the pickle moments. Honestly, it behaved like a feral toddler in a tutu and crooked tiara.

Thank you …

To the ones who called me forward when I wanted to hide.

To the ones who held me when I was falling apart.

To the ones who made me stronger when I was weak.

To the ones who said "write the words" when I wanted to forget it.

To the ones who allowed me to shine and share my light.

To the ones who celebrated me, I celebrate you.

To my clients, past and present, for trusting and allowing me to walk alongside your transformations. You are the reason I do this work.

To my family for your support for my quirks and never-ending creations and ideas.

To Spirit, the Universe, my guides, and that tiny persistent voice that refused to let me quit, I thank you for the nudges, signs, and synchronicities that showed up when I needed them most.

And to you, the reader: May this book find you exactly when you need it and remind you that being a little off kilter is a feature, not a flaw.

Also, to the ones who diminished, disrespected, and dismissed me ... thank you! You are my mirror. And I will continue to be your mirror. This ignited a spark inside me. This journey provided me the opportunity to grow and create the writings to help me overcome my too muchness, not enoughness, and too weirdness. Ultimately having the awareness to recognize that what is coming at me is not meant to define who I am at my core. It is a mirror to elevate me and bring things to my awareness. It is meant to move me from where I am to where I want to be. Which in turn, has allowed me to share with others how to do the same thing.